*GREATER THAN A TOURIST BOOKS ARE
ALSO AVAILABLE IN EBOOK AND
AUDIOBOOK FORMAT.

Greater Than a Tourist
Book Series
Reviews from Readers

I think the series is wonderful and beneficial for tourists to get information before visiting the city.

-Seckin Zumbul, Izmir Turkey

I am a world traveler who has read many trip guides but this one really made a difference for me. I would call it a heartfelt creation of a local guide expert instead of just a guide.

-Susy, Isla Holbox, Mexico

New to the area like me, this is a must have!

-Joe, Bloomington, USA

This is a good series that gets down to it when looking for things to do at your destination without having to read a novel for just a few ideas.

-Rachel, Monterey, USA

D1713835

i

Good information to have to plan my trip to this destination.

-Pennie Farrell, Mexico

Great ideas for a port day.

-Mary Martin USA

Aptly titled, you won't just be a tourist after reading this book. You'll be greater than a tourist!

-Alan Warner, Grand Rapids, USA

Even though I only have three days to spend in San Miguel in an upcoming visit, I will use the author's suggestions to guide some of my time there. An easy read - with chapters named to guide me in directions I want to go.

-Robert Catapano, USA

Great insights from a local perspective! Useful information and a very good value!

-Sarah, USA

This series provides an in-depth experience through the eyes of a local. Reading these series will help you to travel the city in with confidence and it'll make your journey a unique one.

-Andrew Teoh, Ipoh, Malaysia

GREATER THAN A TOURIST- BERMUDA

50 Travel Tips from a Local

Clara Fay

First Edition
Cover designed by: Ivana Stamenkovic
Cover Image: https://pixabay.com/photos/bermuda-ocean-island-boats-sea-
4091370/

CZYK Publishing Since 2011.
CZYKPublishing.com
Greater Than a Tourist
Library of Congress Control Number: 2022907267

Lock Haven, PA

ISBN: 9798437654330

>TOURIST

50 TRAVEL TIPS FROM A LOCAL

BOOK DESCRIPTION

With travel tips and culture in our guidebooks written by a local, it is never too late to visit Bermuda. Greater Than a Tourist - Bermuda by Author Clara Fay offers the inside scoop on the island of Bermuda. Most travel books tell you how to travel like a tourist. Although there is nothing wrong with that, as part of the 'Greater Than a Tourist' series, this book will give you candid travel tips from someone who has lived at your next travel destination. This guide book will not tell you exact addresses or store hours but instead gives you knowledge that you may not find in other smaller print travel books.

Experience cultural, culinary delights, and attractions with the guidance of a Local. Slow down and get to know the people with this invaluable guide. By the time you finish this book, you will be eager and prepared to discover new activities at your next travel destination.

Inside this travel guidebook you will find:

Visitor information from a Local

Tour ideas and inspiration

Valuable guidebook information

Greater Than a Tourist - A Travel Guidebook with 50 Travel Tips from a Local. Slow down, stay in one place, and get to know the people and culture. By the time you finish this book, you will be eager and prepared to travel to your next destination.

OUR STORY

Traveling is a passion of the Greater than a Tourist book series creator. Lisa studied abroad in college, and for their honeymoon Lisa and her husband toured Europe. During her travels to Malta, an older man tried to give her some advice based on his own experience living on the island since he was a young boy. She was not sure if she should talk to the stranger but was interested in his advice. When traveling to some places she was wary to talk to locals because she was afraid that they weren't being genuine. Through her travels, Lisa learned how much locals had to share with tourists. Lisa created the Greater Than a Tourist book series to help connect people with locals. A topic that locals are very passionate about sharing.

TABLE OF CONTENTS

BONUS TIP 1. Watch "Flying Over Bermuda" YouTube Videos

BONUS TIP 2. Apply for a Bermuda Digital Visa: Work from Bermuda Certificate

BONUS TIP 3. Sign Up for BERMUDA. COM Newsletter

TOP REASONS TO BOOK THIS TRIP

Packing and Planning Tips

Travel Questions

Travel Bucket List

NOTES

DEDICATION

I dedicate this book to my partner, who introduced me to distance walking, slow living, and the wonder of early morning birdsong. May the sight of a heron in flight always delight you. May the bluebird song in spring always make you smile. And may you always appreciate the juicy tartness of a Surinam cherry.

Clara Fay

ABOUT THE AUTHOR

Clara Fay was born in Bermuda and spent her childhood enjoying adventures of island life. Returning home several years after attending university in Nova Scotia, she delighted in sharing the unique island experience with her three children and in building a career as a communication professional for a prominent global company.

As do most Bermudians, Clara loves to travel. She especially enjoys exploring the islands of the Scottish Inner and Outer Hebrides, which are so different from her sub-tropical island home. She leveraged her communication expertise to capture the magical, mystical atmosphere, and unique history of those Scottish islands in a recent venture into creative writing with her novel *Mark of a Crescent Moon.* Clara delights in sharing her passion for her island home with this edition of *Greater Than a Tourist - Bermuda.*

When not writing or travelling, Clara appreciates what Bermuda offers, especially outdoor activity. From land to sea, over the years Clara has enjoyed hiking, horseback riding, golf, scuba-diving, swimming, windsurfing, boating, raft ups, deep-sea fishing, sailing, paddle boarding, photography, and most recently pickleball and distance walking. One of her favourite pastimes is spotting herons and their hidden nests.

HOW TO USE THIS BOOK

The *Greater Than a Tourist* book series was written by someone who has lived in an area for over three months. The goal of this book is to help travelers either dream or experience different locations by providing opinions from a local. The author has made suggestions based on their own experiences. Please check before traveling to the area in case the suggested places are unavailable.

Travel Advisories: As a first step in planning any trip abroad, check the Travel Advisories for your intended destination.
https://travel.state.gov/content/travel/en/traveladvisories/traveladvisories.html

FROM THE PUBLISHER

Traveling can be one of the most important parts of a person's life. The anticipation and memories that you have are some of the best. As a publisher of the Greater Than a Tourist, as well as the popular *50 Things to Know* book series, we strive to help you learn about new places, spark your imagination, and inspire you. Wherever you are and whatever you do I wish you safe, fun, and inspiring travel.

Lisa Rusczyk Ed. D.
CZYK Publishing

WELCOME TO
> TOURIST

Bermuda is another world - 700 miles at
sea.
And the way the people greet you - is like a
friendly melody.
To touch a flower in the morning - to listen to
a honeybee.
To hear a bird who sings a song - just to say
that he is free.

Bermuda is another world - turn around, I'll
tell you why.
Just to watch the morning sunrise - from the
sea up to the sky.
Look across at the harbour - see the multi-
coloured sails.
To waterski on the water - that always leaves
a snowy trail.

Bermuda is another world - turn around **and**
you'll be gone.
But there will always be a memory - that will
linger on and on.
And someday I'll hear you say, just as I say
today...
Bermuda is anoooooother woooooorld.

- Hubert Smith, composer of Bermuda's unofficial national anthem,
"Bermuda is Another World."

You can go to heaven if you want to. I'd rather stay in Bermuda.

- Mark Twain

B ermuda is indeed another world, as you'll discover. It's one of those special places that takes you by surprise with its mix of old-world British charm, down-and-real island flavour, and cosmopolitan sophistication.

Just as there are many reasons to travel to Bermuda, whether to relax, immerse in nature, party island style, or have an active adventure, there are many ways to prepare yourself. Some travellers pour over travel guides such as *Fodor's* or *Frommer's,* creating ambitious itineraries of things to do. Other travellers who prefer not to be a "tourist" will seek experiences that help them engage with a new environment like a local. This book gives you focused travel tips from someone who lives in Bermuda.

You will find advice to help you throughout your stay. This book will not provide specifics such as addresses, shop hours, or prices. It will share

11

knowledge, perhaps not found in other smaller print travel books, from someone passionate about their home.

Enjoy Bermuda like a local and discover for yourself why Bermuda is another world.

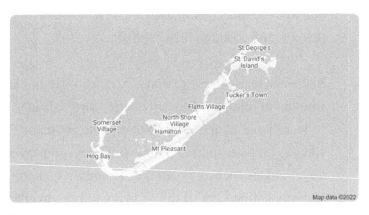

Bermuda

Bermuda Climate

	High	Low
January	70	60
February	69	60
March	70	60
April	72	63
May	76	67
June	82	73
July	85	77
August	86	77
September	85	76
October	80	72
November	75	67
December	72	63

GreaterThanaTourist.com

Temperatures are in Fahrenheit degrees.
Source: NOAA

HOW TO USE THIS BOOK

Authors of the Great Than a Tourist book series have lived in an area for over three months. The goal of the series is to help travellers experience different locations by providing opinions from a local. Suggestions relate to the author's own experiences. Please do your research before travelling to the area in case the suggested places are unavailable. At the end of the list of tips are resources to help you with your further research. Feedback is welcome via email: GreaterThanATouristBermuda@gmail.com.

GOOD TO KNOW THE BASICS

1. WHEN TO VISIT

The archipelago of Bermuda has a mild climate, thanks to the Gulf Stream. This makes for an ideal year-round travel destination. Pick your season to match your purpose.

Winter runs from December through March with air temperature ranging between 65 to 70°F. We focus on New Year's resolutions of fitness and pampering. Events on the calendar include the Goodwill Golf Tournament, the Bermuda Triangle Challenge, Restaurant & Spa Weeks, and the Bermuda Festival of the Performing Arts.

Air temperature climbs to the mid-70s from late March into April as increased sunshine means spring has arrived - along with the cruise ships! We make Easter kites and prepare boats for the fast-approaching summer season. The annual humpback whale migration provides an amazing spectacle best seen from a boat.

The high summer season runs from May through October. Air temperature peaks in July/ August in the 80s and stays there until October. Water sports and outdoor activity are in full swing, as are partying and our favourite social events, such as Bermuda Day, Bermuda Carnival, and Cup Match.

While our busy season may wind down in October, the temperatures don't. Average air temperature in the fall (October/November) remains in the 80s. The difference is that the lower humidity makes the weather perfect for running, cycling, and going to the World Rugby Classic.

For water enthusiasts, the average water temperature in Bermuda roughly follows the changes in air temperature. The water surface temperature ranges from 68°F in the winter months to 82°F in the summer. In November and December, the water temperature averages 73°F.

2. MONEY MATTERS

The Bermuda Dollar ($) is the official currency with a one-to-one ratio with U.S. Dollar. The Bermuda Dollar and the U.S. Dollar are interchangeable. Most retailers and businesses will try to give U.S. Dollar change to visitors.

Canadian dollars, British pounds, and other currencies need to be exchanged at a bank on the island. Banks include HSBC Bank Bermuda Limited, The Bank of N.T. Butterfield & Son Limited, and Clarien Bank Limited.

ATMs are available island wide. You can find 24-hour ATMs at bank branch locations. Also check convenience stores, gas stations, or your hotel. Most ATMs dispense only Bermuda dollars, although HSBC Bank offers U.S. dollars ATMs at their branch locations. Expect to pay fees for the ATM service.

We accept major credit cards, including Visa, MasterCard, and American Express. No U.S. Dollar travel cheques or money orders are accepted.

3. WHERE TO STAY

For an island of 21 square miles, there is a wide selection of accommodations for every taste and budget. There are resort hotels, such as the Cambridge Beaches Resort & Spa and Grotto Bay Beach Resort & Spa. Smaller hotels such as the Royal Palm Hotel and Pompano Beach Club. We have one larger city business hotel, the Hamilton Princess & Beach Club. Bed & breakfast accommodations are available, such as Granaway Guest House & Cottage and Green Bank Guest House & Cottages. AIRBNB and VRBO home sharing options are growing in popularity, such as centrally located Beach Walk Cottages. You should comb through the listings for a place to meet your needs and budget.

Bermuda encompasses nine parishes for administrative purposes. Each parish has its own charm and focus. Your choice of accommodation may come down to location and amenities.

Avid history buffs will enjoy the eastern parish of St. George's. The Town of St. George is a designated UNESCO World Heritage Site. To experience an outstanding example of the earliest English urban settlement in the New World, include the Town of St. George on your itinerary.

Harrington Sound

The eastern/ central parishes of Hamilton, Smith's, and Devonshire, dotted with rolling hills and farmland, have a distinct countryside feel. Harrington Sound in Hamilton Parish is perfect for spotting stingrays, and spending an afternoon at the nearby Bermuda Aquarium, Museum & Zoo. The BQ Beach Grill at John Smith's Bay Beach in Smith's Parish is perfect for lunch on the beach.

The central parish of Pembroke is ideal for those looking to be near the vibrant City of Hamilton, known as Hamilton, and close to shops, restaurants, bars, city parks, museums, galleries, and churches.

The central/ western parishes of Paget, Warwick, Southampton have the famous stretch of pink sand beaches and secluded coves. Stay on the south shore side for proximity to the sand and surf.

Sandy's parish, on the western point of the island, is a good choice for those wishing to get away from the crowds to explore forts, idyllic coves, and the historic Royal Naval Dockyard, known as Dockyard, with its craft market, restaurants, and shopping.

4. GETTING AROUND

Buses and ferries are safe, economical, and allow you to experience our friendly culture. The tall pink air-conditioned buses provide unobstructed views. The ferry routes around the Great Sound or between Hamilton and Dockyard shows Bermuda at its best - from the water.

Motor and pedal bikes, including motor-assisted pedal bikes, are a fun way to explore hidden lanes. Be careful to understand the rules of the road (we drive on the left side). Secure your belongings if using a rear basket.

Rather than conventional car rentals, Bermuda offers eco-friendly, mini two-seater electric cars for hire. This is a more expensive option, but rates vary depending on length of hire. Car formats also vary. There are cars with side-by-side seating, including compact cars or safari style cars, and seating with the passenger directly behind the driver.

Conventional taxi services are available for by-the-hour sightseeing or point-to-point travel. Most taxi vans accommodate 6-7 people. You can raise your hand to hail a taxi, approach the taxi stand on Front Street in Hamilton across from the central flagpole, or phone one of the many taxi providers. Taxi drivers are knowledgeable about the island and happy to answer your questions. If you enjoyed your taxi driver from the airport, get their card to call them while you are on the island.

5. SAY GOOD MORNING

We are approachable and friendly, and love to share information about our island home, but you need to follow one simple rule. When entering a room, climbing onto a bus, passing someone on the street, we greet each other with the appropriate Good Morning/ Afternoon/ Night. If you've lost track of time, "Good Day" will do. Some locals may not interact with you if you don't reciprocate their greeting. If you an employee serving you seems distant, it may be because you've made this honest mistake. Always start with a smile and a greeting when looking for directions. Locals will appreciate that you keep to this custom.

6. BE RESPECTFUL OF THE ENVIRONMENT

The island has no fresh-water lakes, springs, streams, or rivers. We manage our own household water system based on whitewashed rainwater roof catchment and associated storage tanks. We are sensitive to water conservation, especially during months when rainfall is low, and ask our visitors to be mindful of water usage. This explains why we are happy to see a downpour, or "tank rain," in the summer when conditions can be drought-like. Rain should not discourage visitors - it's a reason to celebrate, and it won't last long, anyway.

We respect the environment by cleaning up after ourselves. Certain items are harmful to wildlife, such as plastics, straws, and cigarette butts. Beaches and parks have adequate trash receptacles. There are litter laws in Bermuda with fines up to $2,000.

Another way we respect the environment is to leave nature as we find it. The pink sand of Bermuda beaches is legendary - the colour comes from the crushed skeletons of red foram invertebrates mixed with white limestone sediment. While it's tempting to take home sand or a piece of coral, please refrain from doing so. Instead, take pictures. Photos make the best souvenir, and as the saying goes, a picture is worth a thousand words.

HISTORY AND CULTURE

7. SOAK UP HISTORY IN THE TOWN OF ST. GEORGE

Settled in 1612, the Town of St. George, known as St. George's, is the oldest continuously inhabited town in the Americas. This well-preserved former capital of Bermuda and UNESCO World Heritage Site is the perfect place to discover British colonial architecture, history, and culture.

Get in touch with the past. Wander the charming cobblestone lanes and alleys that have not changed in hundreds of years. Note the unique names that tell of their historic significance, such as Petticoat Lane, Shinbone Alley, Needle & Thread Alley, Featherbed Alley, and Barber's Alley. Run your hands along the limestone walls of buildings and cottages to feel the smoothness of over 400 years of weathering. Visit the St. Peter's Church, the oldest surviving Anglican church in continuous use outside the British Isles and walk through the church graveyard for insight about life in those earliest days. Test out the Stocks & Pillory King's Square for a sense of petty crime punishment. Duck inside the full-sized replica of the

Deliverance on Ordnance Island across from the King's Square to understand the bravery of early settlers crossing the Atlantic in such small vessels.

Seeing St. George's on foot is the best way to immerse in its history. You can join a guided walking tour, hire your own guide, or you may prefer to wander self-guided.

Guided walking tours are a great way to gain insight and answers for your burning questions. Certified walking tour guides will take you to important landmarks and historical sites. Call or visit the Bermuda Visitor Services Centre - St. George's on York Street for contact information on guided walking tours.

For something a little different, book a Haunted History Tour with storytellers dressed in period costumes who take you through the narrow lanes and winding alleys after dark.

If you prefer self-guided walking, stop in at the Bermuda Visitor Services Centre - St. George's to pick up information brochures and maps of the historic town.

8. HAMILTON WALKING TOUR WITH TOWN CRIER ED CHRISTOPHER

From April through December, the City of Hamilton offers free Discover Hamilton walking tours with Town Crier Ed Christopher, one of Bermuda's most well-known and knowledgeable figures. Our Town Crier shares information gleaned from over 25 years on the job, extensive research, and oral stories passed down for generations about the colourful history of Hamilton. Walk-ins are welcome, but it is best to book by emailing or phoning the City of Hamilton.

Our Town Crier also offers private tours for groups, and for special occasions. The North Hamilton Bar Hopping Tour allows you to mingle with residents of this vibrant corner of Hamilton by visiting a series of bars including Place's, Spinning Wheel, Legends

Sports Bar, and more. This tour encourages responsible drinking. You should arrange adequate transportation to get you safely to your next destination. You must be of Legal Drinking Age, which is 18 years old and over in Bermuda, to join this tour. Email towncrier@cityhall.bm to book a private group tour, or the North Hamilton Bar Hopping Tour with Town Crier Ed Christopher.

9. BERMUDA NATIONAL TRUST OFFERS CREATIVE LEARNING EXPERIENCES

The Bermuda National Trust is a registered charity organisation dedicated to preserving Bermuda's natural and cultural heritage by acquiring and conserving land, buildings, and artifacts, and inspiring stewardship through advocacy, and education. While focused on advocating Bermuda for Bermudians, the Bermuda National Trust has much to offer visitors who wish to enhance their appreciation of the history, culture, and natural beauty of the island through creative learning experiences.

For a flavour of Bermuda architecture and way of life, visit one of the Trust's four flagship houses and garden properties open to the public. The properties display a range of Bermudian art, furniture, silver, china, and curiosities: the Waterville Historic House, Park and Gardens is close to Hamilton on Pomander Road in Paget; Tucker House Historic Home and Museum is in St. George's on Water Street; Verdmont Historic Home and Garden is in Smith's Parish; and the Globe House Museum is on Duke of York Street in St. George's.

To venture into the unusual, visit one of Bermuda's 14 beautiful historic cemeteries. The Trust leases and cares for many of the historic cemeteries with the support of the Commonwealth War Graves Commission and the Canadian War Graves Commission. The headstones and engravings give you a sense of life in those earlier years. Dedicated craft-workers keep the memorials in good repair.

Check the Bermuda National Trust website for opening hours. You can download a map of Trust properties across the island that are open to the public, including historic buildings, nature reserves, wetlands, and historic cemeteries. The Trust also sponsors activities that visitors can join, such as the famous 5-mile Palm Sunday Walk through historic areas. You can call or visit their Waterville head office to ask questions and get information on how you can best enjoy what the Bermuda National Trust offers.

10. GOMBEYS AND FESTAS

There are no true native people in Bermuda. The people who live here had roots in other countries. We are proud to trace our ancestors to the Caribbean, Europe, South America, and Africa.

We celebrate our diversity through what we share as a community. Mostly we share a love of our island home, music, and spirited fun - Bermuda style.

Two of our much-loved Bermudian traditions come from other islands where our people originated. The Gombeys are a cultural icon reflecting Bermuda's blend of West Indian, African, Native American, and British cultures. Festas reflect Bermuda's Portuguese heritage, originating from the islands of Madeira and the Azores.

While there are similar Gombey-style traditions in various Caribbean islands, the UNESCO Cultural and Conservation Conference in 1970 recognised Bermuda's Gombey dancers as a unique Bermudian art form. Resplendent in vivid coloured costumes with tall peacock-feathered headdresses and dramatic capes that are unique for each Gombey, the troupes will have you dancing on the spot with rhythmic drumming, whistling, and theatrics. We can find Gombey dancers in a variety of venues, including the Harbour Nights Street Festival during the summer months, and the Bermuda Day Parade in May, among others. Check with the Visitor Service Centre - Hamilton for more information on venues.

In May, the Portuguese Community in Bermuda organises an annual festival (Festa do Senhor Santo

Cristo dos Milagres) to celebrate the Holy Spirit. This is a tradition that started in the Azores over 100 years ago. The community gathers for a parade, music, traditional folk dancing, and Portuguese food. All are welcome to join this cultural street festival.

11. EASTER WEEKEND TRADITIONS

Easter weekend is a great time to visit Bermuda. The buzz of spring is in the air, as is the humming of homemade Bermuda kites.

We celebrate Easter weekend with colourful homemade kites, sunrise service on the shore, codfish cakes served on hot cross buns, and fragrant Bermuda Easter lilies to decorate our homes.

Sign up for a traditional Bermuda kite-making workshop, and then join hundreds of locals flying homemade kites at various locations on Good Friday. Horseshoe Bay, Astwood Park, the Botanical Gardens, and Shelly Bay Park are popular locations for kite flying. The Bermuda Society of the Arts hosts a kite-making workshop on the Saturday before Good Friday.

For information on sunrise services on the shore, contact St. Paul's Church in Paget and Christ Church in Warwick. Churches and religious communities in Bermuda provide schedules of services on their websites.

You can purchase Bermuda style codfish cakes and hot cross buns across the island during the week before Easter weekend at places like Miles, the Market Place, Harrington Hundreds, and most grocery stores and bakeries.

Field of Bermuda Easter Lilies in Smith's Parish

The Bermuda Easter lily is one of the finest flowering plants introduced into Bermuda. Between 1927 and 1941, sixty-seven percent of the total acreage of Bermuda lilies grew on St. David's Island. Bermudians and visitors would take a trip by horse-drawn carriage or bicycle to see the lilies in full bloom. Today, one of the most expansive fields of Bermuda Easter lilies is on the corner of Middle Road and Watlington Road East in Smith's Parish. Stop to take a photo of the lilies in the field in full bloom. You can purchase Bermuda Easter lilies from garden nurseries, grocery stores, and many roadside stands, such as at the corner mentioned above.

12. BERMUDA DAY WEEKEND

We observe our national Bermuda Day holiday on the final Friday before the end of May. This holiday is a time to celebrate our unique cultural heritage. Bermuda Day marks the official start of summer. No self-respecting Bermudian would think to swim, or wear Bermuda shorts, before Bermuda Day.

Bermuda Day kicks off with the Bermuda Day Half Marathon Derby, Bermuda's longest standing race, dating back to 1909. Every year, the marathon attracts hundreds of spectators who line the streets from Somerset to Bernard's Park to cheer the runners on. Visitors are welcome to sign up for the marathon, though they are not eligible to win prizes for race performance. Check out www.Bermudamarathon.bm to sign up.

During the Bermuda Day holiday, people sporting BBQs, coolers, tents, tables, and chairs line the streets of Hamilton. People spend the entire day watching the half-marathoners run through Hamilton to the finish line, and then they watch the Bermuda Day Parade with its pageantry of floats, bands, and traditional Gombey dancers.

13. CUP MATCH IS MORE THAN CRICKET

Cup Match is a two-day public holiday celebrating Emancipation Day. We hold the annual holiday on the Thursday and Friday in July closest to August 1st. Unique to the island of Bermuda, our national Cup Match holiday is a time to enjoy camping, boating, swimming, partying, and, of course, cricket.

The Cup Match cricket game pits rival teams from the west end against the east end. Weeks before the game, fans support their team by dressing in team colours - red and navy for Somerset and pale blue and dark blue for St. George's. The venue changes every year as each team takes turns hosting.

The Cup Match cricket field is famous for its festival spirit. Families pitch camps to be comfortable while enjoying the two-day event. This is a great place to try local cuisine, including mussel pie, shark-hash, fried fish, beef pie, and conch. There is also a good measure of rum swizzle at hand. Try your luck at the dice game Crown & Anchor, a strictly controlled gambling game played legally only at Cup Match. With roots dating back to the 18th century when the British Royal Navy was based in Bermuda, Crown & Anchor is a much-anticipated tradition at Cup Match.

Visitors are welcome at Cup Match and will find locals happy to explain the nuances of the game and provide guidance on the best local favourite refreshments to enjoy.

OUT AND ABOUT

14. IN THE WATER

The water around Bermuda is clean and welcoming. It's hard to resist jumping into the brilliant turquoise crystal-clear water for a swim, especially on humid days. Average water temperature is temperate, which is good for year-round water activities.

Bermuda's famous pink sand beaches are alluring. There are beaches for everyone. Whether you love sand & surf, or sand & calm water, Bermuda has a great selection of choices. Even if you don't like sand, there are many places to enjoy a warm, salty, therapeutic swim.

Horseshoe Bay in one of the must-see stretches of shoreline. Stroll to the far eastern end of the beach to explore secluded coves and rock formations. Climb the rock cliff at the western end of the beach for an amazing view and great photo spot. Turn right at the main entrance of Horseshoe Bay to find Port Royal Cove, known as the baby beach, a perfect sheltered, shallow calm water area for small children. With amenities such as beach equipment rentals, a

restaurant and bar, and facilities, Horseshoe Bay
makes for an easy and fun day at the beach.

Port Royal Cove at Horseshoe Bay

Other popular surf & sand beaches for swimming
include John Smith's Bay in Smith's Parish, Elbow
Beach in Paget, Warwick Long Bay in Warwick, and
Church Bay and West Whale Bay, both in
Southampton.

For sand & calm shallow waters, go to Clearwater
Beach and Turtle Bay in St. David's past the L.F.
Wade Airport. Tourists rarely visit these side-by-side
beaches because of their distance from Hamilton.

We come on the weekends for family picnics and BBQs. Between the two beaches, there is a big shade tree perfect for picnics off the sand, with access to a quick dip after lunch. Beyond Turtle Bay, which as the name suggests is a great turtle-spotting area, is Cooper's Island Nature Reserve. You'll find some of the most pristine and secluded beaches there. Motor vehicles are forbidden past the barrier at the entrance, which makes taking picnic baskets, coolers, and other beach paraphernalia difficult. This is a place of beauty for those travelling light. Long Bay Beach on the south-eastern shore of Cooper's Island, fringed by palm trees, is picture perfect.

View of Turtle Bay

Love the water, but don't like the sand? Spanish Point Park, 15 minutes from Hamilton, is a quiet neighbourhood favourite. When you arrive, you may see a few locals sitting in the parking lot chatting, enjoying the view, perhaps playing cards or dominoes. Turn right past the turnstile to find water access to a shallow, sandy bottom swimming area in front of two small islands. Straight ahead at the point is a splendid view of Dockyard. Steps carved out of the rocks on the right provide water access. If you want to pick up snacks on your way to the park, stop at M Soares and Son grocery store on Spanish Point Road on the left less than a quarter of a mile from the park entrance.

Spanish Point

Other popular no-sandy beach swimming places include Deep Bay/ Clarence Cove at Admiralty House Park in Pembroke, and Ferry Point Park in St. George's.

You can swim from just about any place on the island. Always carry one of those quick-drying microfiber camping towels with you. Self-touring by bike or electric mini car is perfect for pulling over at a safe spot and jumping into the water. There are suitable lay-bys along our roads, such as Theo's Cove on Cockburn Road before entering the Dockyard. Be sure before you take a leap off higher cliffs and rocks, like at Admiralty House Park where we go cliff jumping, or public docks, such as Harrington Sound Public dock, to ensure the water is sufficiently deep for your plunge, and that there are no dangerous rocks hidden in the water. Also, check for a safe and easy way back on land.

15. ON THE WATER

Whether you're a fan of fast-paced adventure, exhilarating water sports, or an easy glide over the sea, you can enjoy a full range of activity on the water.

Jet skiing gives a different perspective from the calm waters of the inner sounds and is just plain fun. There are several jet ski rental companies offering different packages and various starting points and routes. Check out K.S. Watersports and Bermuda Watersports for jet ski tours and combination packages with snorkelling and jet skiing.

Kite surfing has grown in popularity in recent years at Elbow Beach, Shelly Bay Beach, Somerset Long Bay, and Horseshoe Bay, depending on the wind direction. Bermuda's wind is most consistent from December through May, but the water temperature is cool, so wear a wetsuit. For rentals and instruction, check out Island Winds.

Nothing beats Church Bay and Tobacco Bay for snorkelling. Church Bay is a small beach with a system of shallow reefs close to shore that nurture an abundance of marine life and protect snorkelers from breakers. There are no facilities at Church Bay. Tobacco Bay is a shallow, calm water bay surrounded by interesting limestone formations that protect marine life. Tobacco Bay boasts a family-friendly restaurant and great beverages. You can rent snorkel equipment and paddle boards during the high season from April until December. The beach is open to the public all year.

Limestone Formations at Tobacco Bay

Kayaking and paddle boarding around the inlets and coves of Bermuda is relaxing. Check out Blue Hole Watersports at Grotto Bay for equipment rental and guided tours explore Whalebone Bay, Walsingham Nature Reserve, and Bailey's Bay from the water.

We have over 300 shipwrecks around the island, some being shallow water wrecks at 30 feet. Most are between 30 and 70 feet. National Geographic designated Bermuda as one of the top nine dive destinations in the world. Water visibility ranges from 70 to 100 feet with the occasional 150-foot day. Safety and instruction standards are high, and you can find certified dive shops island wide. Check out Blue Water Divers & Watersports, Dive Bermuda, a PADI centre at Grotto Bay, and Fantasea Diving & Watersports at Dockyard.

Other popular water sports such as parasailing, windsurfing, boating, and sailing are widely available on the island.

16. FISHING YOUR WAY

Fishing is a year-round sport in Bermuda. Peak season runs from May to November when seas are calm and big fish like wahoo, tuna, and Mahi-Mahi run in large schools offshore. For the best chance to capture a big blue marlin, plan your trip between June and September.

For reef and deep-sea fishing, charter a boat from an experienced captain. He will know the best places to fish and the best techniques to land your prized big one. You should not expect to bring home all your catch since many captains supplement their income by selling the fish to restaurants and markets.

Shore fishing for snapper, triggerfish, porgies, pompano, bonefish, and barracuda can be rewarding. This type of fishing does not require a license or permit. Look for large expanses of shallow water along the shore, such as Harrington Sound, Daniel's Head, Castle Harbour, and Devonshire Bay.

17. WALK, HIKE, OR MOUNTAIN BIKE BERMUDA'S RAILWAY TRAIL

Spanning the island from end to end, the Bermuda Railway Trail, which operated from 1931 to 1948 as the island's primary means of transportation, was updated in 1984 and is a perfect off-road trail for walkers and cyclists.

The Railway Trail feels like countryside. The trail provides a unique perspective of Bermuda that you will remember, especially if you complete the entire trail. (See the Bermuda End-to-End organised charity event in May.) You can walk, run, or cycle the trail, though if you cycle, you will need to lift your cycle over a few low stiles intended to stop motorbikes from accessing the trails. An electric motor assisted pedal cycle may be an option to help you complete the entire Railway Trail.

The Railway Trail shows parts of Bermuda you may not otherwise see, like the wild cliffs of the east end coast, the lush tree tunnels of the central parishes, the sweeping views of the Great Sound in Southampton, and the rich farmlands all along the trail.

See nature's bounty and Bermuda's gorgeous flora. In late February and early March, look out for ripe Loquat fruit, with its flavour of cherry, apricot, and plum. Surinam cherries ripen from April to early June. Fresh picked Loquat fruit and Surinam cherries are a tasty treat. In September and October, you may see night-blooming cereus cactus flowers.

You'll need to go off the trail at points where it's not connected. Most of the trail from Paget to Somerset is continuous.

Plan your itinerary in advance. Take periodic rest stops, take snacks and water, and plan how to return home. If you walk toward Dockyard, you can return to Hamilton on the Ferry, and you can bring pedal cycles or motor assisted pedal cycles onboard. Dockyard has many pubs and restaurants to enjoy at the end of your adventure. Check out the Railway Trail website for a trail map and itinerary.

18. THE NATURAL WONDER OF CAVES

The island is comprised of a thick layer of marine limestone capping an extinct submerged volcanic mountain range and fringed by coral reefs. Like many places where limestone is the dominant bedrock, we have a network of caves. The greatest concentration of caves is around Harrington Sound in some of the island's oldest rock formations. General tourists can explore some caves. Many are underwater and only accessible by divers. Always take sensible precautions when exploring caves.

Crystal Cave and Fantasy Cave are must-see attractions. The natural underground beauty of the stalagmites and stalactites surrounding the bright blue water is stunning. Guided tours leave every 20 minutes and there is a combined rate if you want to view both caves. Plan your excursion around lunch to enjoy a fish sandwich at the outdoor Cafe Olé next to the cave entrance.

Cathedral and Prospero Caves are on the grounds of the Grotto Bay Hotel Resort. Grotto Bay has created a unique cave spa experience. For a special treat, call or email the hotel to book a spa appointment at their spa cave.

There are caves to explore on your own, with sensible precaution. Admiral's Cave, one of the largest dry caves in Bermuda, is on Henry's Hill in Hamilton Parish. You'll also come across caves while exploring the Walsingham Nature Reserve, a lush and interesting forest trail known to locals as Tom Moore's Jungle.

Admiralty House Park at Spanish Point in Pembroke has a system of tunnels and artificial caves constructed in the 1800s by the British military. A friend hosted a surprise birthday party inside the main cave on the western side, and it was an atmospheric event never to be forgotten.

If you prefer to explore exclusive and secluded caves with a guide, check out tour companies such as Hidden Gems of Bermuda Ltd.

19. CATCH A SUNRISE FROM THE BEACH

Nothing beats the kaleidoscope of colours of an island sunset, especially as seen from the water's edge with your feet in the sand. Except for a sunrise. The theatrics of the sun rising from the ocean are spectacular, especially on a cloudy morning. Turn around to see the colours bouncing in the sky towards the west.

One of the best positioned beaches to watch a sunrise is Grape Bay Beach in Paget, named for the bay grape trees surrounding it. This secluded beach, with its interesting combination of sand flats and rock pools to explore, is a private beach accessible only by residents of the four roads leading to the beach. Tourists staying in accommodations on those roads, such as Beach Walk Apartments and Grape Bay Studio Apartment on White Sands Road, can access Grape Bay Beach.

East facing public beaches best suited for experiencing the splendid Bermuda sunrises are St. Catherine's Beach, John Smith's, and Elbow Beach.

DINING AND BEVERAGES

20. LOCAL FAVOURITES

The varied flavours of our island food match our heritage as a people. You'll find restaurants catering to every palate. We have our Bermudian specialties and love to talk about them. Discussion about where to find the best of our favourites is a national pastime.

We consider the Bermuda fish chowder as our national dish. Its basic ingredients are fish, tomatoes, and onions, seasoned with black rum and a Bermuda-created "sherry peppers sauce," which you can purchase to take home. Wait staff will bring bottles of black rum and sherry peppers sauce to the table so you can add the amount you want to your chowder. Most restaurants island-wide include Bermuda fish chowder on their menu, so it might be fun to try a few places to discover your favourite. In Hamilton, try the Bermuda fish chowder at Hog Penny on Burnaby Street, the Lobster Pot & Boathouse Bar on Bermudiana Road, and Astwood Arms on Front Street. In St. George's, try the chowder at Wahoo's Bistro & Patio on Water Street.

Let's talk pie. Individual portion pies. Fish pie, mussel pie, chicken pie, beef pie, lamb pie, vegetable pie - seasoned with curry and enjoyed our way, with a healthy blob of mayonnaise. In Hamilton, go to the Pie Factory at Parliament St. In St. George's, stop for a savoury treat at the Bermuda Pie Company at Wellington Slip Rd. Most grocery stores carry hot Bermuda pies in a heating rack.

The Bermuda fish sandwich is our national obsession. Periodic competitions set out to resolve the question of where to find the best ones. Lightly battered and seasoned fried local fish is slathered with homemade tartar sauce, loaded with coleslaw, and placed between slices of raisin bread. Art Mel's Spicy Dicy, known as Art Mel's, is the mecca for fish sandwich fans. Their fish sandwiches are huge, perfectly prepared, and a great value. Art Mel's is off the beaten path just outside Hamilton, so ask for directions. In the west end, Woody's Sports Bar & Restaurant is a locals' hangout that few tourists know about. We queue at the outside counter for takeout, then dive into a great fish sandwich and beverage at one of the picnic tables on the patio and enjoy the ocean view.

The term dark and stormy does not refer to the weather. Goslings Dark 'n' Stormy®, a trademarked highball cocktail with an interesting maritime history, is made with Goslings Black Seal® rum and Goslings Stormy Ginger Beer®, served over ice, and garnished with a slice of lime. Rum Swizzle is another island favourite, and you'll find many recipe variations. Go to the Swizzle Inn Pub & Restaurant in Bailey's Bay, known as the Swizzle, Bermuda's oldest pub, to understand why it's known as home to the Bermuda Rum Swizzle. The Swizzle, of "swizzle in, swagger out" t-shirt fame, is our favourite stop on the way to the airport when we send off our visitors.

Now you're armed to discuss Bermuda's favourite foods and beverages with your taxi driver!

21. ALFRESCO DINING WATERSIDE

There's nothing quite as delightful as enjoying a meal in the open air beside to the ocean. With warm ocean breezes, ready access to the water, and no pesky insects to bother you, outdoor dining waterside is perfect in Bermuda.

In Hamilton, the Harbourfront Restaurant offers upscale dining on a dock with a clear west-facing view of Hamilton harbour. Be sure to time your reservation to catch the sunset. For more casual dining, several locations in St. George's have terraces and patios within a few feet of the water. You can feed the parrot fish swimming beside you at Wahoo's Bistro & Patio, the White Horse Pub & Restaurant, and the Wharf. Cafe Lido and Mickey's Bistro in Paget offer both fine dining and casual dining, beach-side. Further afield in Southampton, relax to the sound of crashing waves at Coconuts, the open-air restaurant built into the rock face above the beach at the Reefs Resort & Club.

Do you dream of dining with white linen table service while your toes dig into warm sand? Your best bet is to check out the Reefs Resort & Club, the Hamilton Princess & Beach Club, and Cambridge Beaches Resort & Spa.

22. RAISE A GLASS

With global spirits' giant Bacardi Limited headquartered in Bermuda, and with Gosling Brothers Ltd., of Goslings Black Seal rum fame, established in Bermuda in 1806, it's small wonder the island has a robust cocktail and highball scene.

Friday night in Bermuda is about the Happy Hour. We pour out of office buildings and other places of employment and head to our favourite bars and pubs for the company of friends and a relaxing beverage. Saturday night is for events, "date night," and hanging out at home. Any night of the week is good for Bermuda's bar scene.

For upscale cocktail bars in Hamilton, Port O Call Restaurant, Harry's at the Waterfront, and Barracuda Grill are winners. In Warwick, Blu Bar and Grill at Newstead Belmont Hills Golf Course is worth the trip. The Conservatory Bar & Lounge of the Rosewood Bermuda Resort on Tuckers Point Drive is truly sophisticated.

Watch your favourite game in the company of fellow fans at one of our great sports bars. Just remember, we call it "football" and not "soccer." In Hamilton, go to Flanagan's Outback Sports Bar, Docksider Pub & Restaurant where rugby is the game of choice, and Robin Hood Pub & Restaurant. At the Turtle Hills Golf Course in Southampton, Boundary Sports Bar & Grille has many large screens and serves substantial bar food and beverages.

For inexpensive highballs and lively conversation, try Place's Place and the Spinning Wheel Night Club in North Hamilton. Blue Water Anglers Club & Bar, on the outskirts of Hamilton, also serves reasonably priced highballs. On Friday night, locals go to the Blue Water Anglers for a fish fry, enjoyed on the dock. The bar at Wahoo's Bistro & Patio is famous for comradery that spills onto the alley, and where the bar's owners join you for a shooter of your favourite spirit.

As the oldest remaining British Overseas Territory, Bermuda has its share of British-style pubs. Top on the list is the island's oldest pub, the Swizzle, famous for its atmosphere, live entertainment, originality in pub food, selection of ales, beer, and cocktails, and restaurant walls graffitied with business cards and dollar bills. The Hog Penny, opened in 1957, is Hamilton's oldest licensed establishment and serves authentically local and British pub favourites. The Frog & Onion Pub and Restaurant, housed in the mid-18th century Cooperage in historic Dockyard, makes eight varieties of beers and ales in its own microbrewery onsite, using a British style of brewing. The Astwood Arms in Hamilton offers a modern twist on a Victorian era style pub combined with a sport bar atmosphere.

23. WINE AND SPIRITS TASTINGS

In Bermuda, we love to experiment and learn about wine and spirits. The best way is with guidance from a trained brand ambassador.

Bacardi Limited owns Bacardí rum, Grey Goose vodka, Dewar's Scotch whisky, Bombay gin, Martini vermouth, and Patrôn tequila to name a few, and has a Bermuda-resident brand ambassador who hosts monthly spirits tasting and learning sessions. Visitors are welcome to attend and should book ahead. Follow the Bacardi Bermuda brand ambassador on social media - @TheBacardiGuy. He is "shaking it up in Bermuda."

Gosling Brothers Limited is a Bermuda company that manufactures and distributes rum and imports and distributes wine and spirits. The company maintains a retail presence on the island. For information on tasting sessions and events, check their social media - @goslingslimitedbda and @goslingsrum. You can book Gosling's Rum

Tasting Cruises, offered in the high season, through the Island Tour Centre.

The Tasting Room in Devonshire has a dedicated tasting room for walk-in tastings, using wine dispensers. Private group tasting sessions of 2 to 20 people can be booked ahead by phone or email. The Tasting Room also offers ticketed events. Follow them on social media - @TheTastingRoomBDA - or sign up on their website for their weekly newsletter.

Most wine retailers periodically host wine tasting sessions. Check out the Bermuda events calendar and plug into social media to find out when they are offered.

24. CONVENIENT PREPARED FOOD FOR THOSE IN HOME SHARES

One reason you may choose accommodation with a kitchen is for the ease of preparing your own meals or getting takeaway. Sometimes you just don't want to eat out for every meal. There are many options for convenient prepared food.

Several groceries have fresh daily buffets. The Hamilton Marketplace on Church Street is one of the more popular buffets, boasting an extensive range of breakfast and lunch food, which you can, of course, use for dinner. The Hamilton Marketplace posts daily menus online, with a daily selection of prepared sushi and grab-and-go sandwiches. The Supermart on Front Street focuses on fresh Bermudian cuisine on its buffet. They also bring in fresh Waitrose's cooked food from the United Kingdom, a great option for heat-and-serve meals. Miles Market at the Waterfront on Pitts Bay Road provides more upmarket food, either prepared from Miles-to-go or ready-prepped from the deli for cooking at home. Check out their website for daily menus.

Most island restaurants provide takeaway service. Take the guesswork out of wondering how you're going to pick up the food by using the island's main home delivery service, Sargasso Sea Ltd. Bermuda. See the many restaurants, bars, and shops partnered with the Sargasso Sea home delivery service on their website, or download their app.

Many grocery stores offer home delivery service. The MarketPlace chain of grocery stores provides widespread home delivery throughout the island.

If you have a plant-based lifestyle you'd like to continue while on holiday, then Nourished Bermuda meals are for you. Nourished Bermuda offers economical, locally sourced plant-based prepared meals to store in the fridge or freezer until ready to reheat and eat. With a little planning, you can place your Nourished Bermuda order before you arrive on the island, pick up your order, and enjoy a week of meals your way. For order cut-off and pick up information, along with order details, see the Nourished Bermuda website.

Fresh Bermuda fish is available from our local fishers, cleaned and ready to cook. There are roadside stands all around the island to purchase fish fresh fish and chat with the fishers. Close to Hamilton, check out Vitamin Sea Fisheries fish stand at the top of Trimingham Hill before the South Shore roundabout. M Soares and Son grocery store is well-stocked with fresh Bermuda fish.

25. GREAT PICNIC SPOTS

We love to picnic in Bermuda. There is nothing as relaxing as a shady picnic with family and friends.

If you like to picnic on the grass under a shady tree, try the Bermuda Botanical Gardens, the Arboretum, Victoria Park, and Par-la-Ville Park. Victoria Park has a food truck selling desserts, and Par-La-Ville Park has a vendor selling boba tea.

For picnic spots with ocean views, Astwood Cove Park, Spanish Point Park, Clearwater Beach, and Ferry Point Park near the Martello Tower Fort are for you. The bus stop lay-by just before Church Bay has picnic tables, perfect for pulling off the road for a quick snack and a splendid view.

Picnic spot at lay-by overlooking Church Bay

Beach picnics are an essential part of island life. Just about any beach is perfect for a picnic, such as Church Bay, Cooper's Island Nature Reserve, Clearwater Beach, and Whale Bay.

For picnics on the water, there are boat charter operators who provide lovely meals on board sailing or motor vessels to top off your water experience.

You can fill up your "picnic basket" from grocery store aisles, including the prepared food buffets mentioned above, or you can order takeaway. For those who want a truly unique, charming, and upscale experience, Eettafel is a boutique events company that can create a luxury, rustic style picnic experience for your pleasure.

THE "GO TO" LOCAL EVENTS

26. PARTY LIKE A LOCAL AT CARNIVAL

We hold the Bermuda Carnival on the third weekend of June, which is a public holiday known as Bermuda Heroes Weekend celebrating Bermuda's national heroes. The Carnival draws inspiration from Caribbean carnivals such as the Trinidad and Tobago Carnival and Barbados Crop Over, while celebrating unique elements of the Bermudian culture. The Bermuda Carnival is one of the fastest growing carnivals in the world.

Carnival is all about live music concerts and entertainment, lots of street parties/fetes, an all-night J'ouvert celebration, delicious local cuisine, boat rides, Raft Up, and so much more.

Five Star Friday kicks off the weekend, with live performances and the best local and international DJs and soca artists.

Early Saturday morning is J'ouvert, meaning "dawn/daybreak" in some of the French-creole based languages of the Caribbean. J'ouvert is the wildest fete to take place under the moonlight, ending at dawn when party-goers head home to shower off the colour dust and glitter sprayed on them during J'ouvert.

At noon on Saturday, Carnival takes to the water for Raft Up - one of the largest boats raft up parties of the year. A floating barge serves as the stage for performers. You must come by boat or other floating devices to attend this event. There are boat tour operators you can book to take you to experience Raft Up.

The weekend culminates on Monday afternoon with Parade of Bands. Troupes dressed in elaborate costumes, some with elaborate headdresses, parade along a designated route, normally through Hamilton. You can be a spectator, or you can take part. To join as a participant, sign up with a Mas Band in advance. For information about Mas Band, check out the Bermuda Carnival site on Carnivaland.net. Click on the links for each individual Mas Band's information. Follow Bermuda Carnival on social media - @BermudaCarnival.

27. PONY HARNESS RACING

Pony Harness Racing in Bermuda, where horses pull two-wheeled carts, is more demanding than anywhere else in the world because of the size and shape of the Vesey Street racetrack in Devonshire. Races take place from September to May, in the evenings or on Sunday afternoons. Facilities at the racetrack include a show ring, a canteen, spectator stands, and parking. This is a fun outing for the entire family.

28. PARTY ON THE BEACH

Relax by day, party by night. The beach is an atmospheric place for a party in the evening, especially under a moonlight.

Tobacco Bay is the beach party to join on Friday nights during the high season, with live music, happy hour specials, and roaring bonfires. On Monday nights, Snorkel Park Beach transforms from snorkelling by day to partying by night with DJs and live music.

On Christmas morning, hundreds of locals, ex-pats, and visitors go to Elbow Beach for a sunrise champagne salute. The sight and sounds of hundreds of people swathed in festive colours popping champagne bottles are sure to make your Christmas merry and bright. Bring your own bottle to join the party.

Many of the resorts and larger hotels also host parties on the beach, so check out their websites for information.

29. BERMUDA FITTED DINGHY RACES

The Bermuda Fitted Dinghy is a racing-dedicated sailboat used in competitions fought between the Royal Bermuda Yacht Club (RBYC), the Royal Hamilton Amateur Dinghy Club (RHADC), the St.

George's Dinghy & Sports Club, and the Sandys Boat Club.

Singularly awkward looking in design, with a hull measuring exactly 14'1" and seating a crew of six or seven, the Bermuda Fitted Dinghy is one of the world's most amazing sailboats. Unique to this racing is the strategic jettisoning of crew, which risks being unable to keep the boat upright. Boats often sink in one race, then get bailed and sail to victory in a later race the same day.

The racing schedule sets dates between May and September in a variety of locations, including Hamilton or St. George's Harbours, Granaway Deep, and Mangrove Bay. It's best to view the Bermuda Fitted Dinghy Races from the water. To rent a boat, book well in advance. It's important to be a competent boat operator to deal with the flotilla of spectator boats in and around the races.

30. JOIN BERMUDA'S LARGEST RAFT UP

On the Sunday after Cup Match, head to Mangrove Bay in Somerset. You will find the largest and wildest raft up parties on the island there. Practically every boat registered in Bermuda shows up at Mangrove Bay for this end of Cup Match event. Join the party on the beach. Take anything that floats with you. Don't forget your cooler. Alternatively, book a spot on any of the tour boats heading for Mangrove Bay, such as the ÜberVida, one of the island's most popular party boats.

THE SPORTING LIFE

31. NAME YOUR SPORT

18th Hole at Five Forts Golf Course in St. George's

Bermuda is a haven for outdoor recreational sports. Whether passionate about golf, tennis, pickleball, sailing, or running, we enjoy our choice of outdoor sports year-round.

We are fortunate to have more golf courses in Bermuda per square mile than anywhere else in the world; all with stunning views and unique challenges. Turtle Hill Golf Club, ranked one of the top five par 3 courses in the world by *Golf*

Magazine, is perfect for all skill levels. Mid Ocean Club stresses the long game with six par 4s over 400 yards. Ocean View Golf Course, a nine-hole course with a four-star rating by *Golf Digest*, has some steep fairways that are fun to play. Port Royal Golf Course is the longest and most picturesque course in Bermuda and hosted the PGA Grand Slam Championship for seven consecutive years. Newstead Belmont Hills features tiered greens and narrow fairways, making it interesting for all handicaps. Tucker's Point Golf Course, one of the oldest on the island, is on the world's innovative list of golf courses following a course redesign. Five Forts Golf Club is a friendly par-62 course perfect for beginners and experts alike.

If tennis is your game, you can book a court at many resorts and smaller hotels across the island. A few home share options include tennis courts. If that is important to you, add it to your accommodation search criteria. The Pomander Gate Tennis Club welcomes visitors and offers a reasonable weekly temporary membership. Interested persons should contact the Pomander Gate office.

The least expensive option is the Government-run W.E.R. Joell Tennis Stadium just minutes from Hamilton. Call the number on the Bermuda Lawn Tennis Association website for court bookings. www.blta.bm.

Pickleball grew in 2021 to 4.8 million players in the United States alone. In Bermuda, we're seeing the game become increasingly popular, and there are a handful of places where you can play. Pompano Beach Club allows non-guests access to play on their pickleball courts. Call ahead to book your court. The pickleball courts at the Hamilton Princess & Beach Club are only available for guests and members of the resort. For those seeking home share options, Banstead has a tennis/ pickleball court for use by their guests and guests staying at Beach Walk Cottages. Pomander Gate Tennis Club, the club that first introduced pickleball to the island, offers a reasonable weekly temporary membership. Interested persons should contact the Pomander Gate office.

Bermuda continues to be a worldwide favourite spot for yachting and sailing. Whether you rent a sailboat to explore the many islets, reefs, marine life, and shipwrecks, or hire a tour operator to show you the sights, sailing is a very pleasant way to enjoy the natural beauty of Bermuda.

You should choose your location carefully for running. The roads are narrow and lacking good shoulders or walkways. From Elbow Beach along South Shore to the Hamilton Princess in Hamilton, you'll find a continuous sidewalk about 3.5 miles long, which is safe to run. You'll find a combination of beaches, sandy dunes, and wider roads with sweeping views of the south shore coast along the stretch between Elbow Beach and Horseshoe Bay. The best off-road running is the Bermuda Railway Trail with its hard-packed soil surface. Other good off-road options include trails in the Botanical Gardens, the Arboretum, and South Shore Park.

32. CALLING ALL BIRDERS

Sandpipers on Horseshoe Bay

Bermuda is ideal for bird lovers. Our isolated location in the North Atlantic attracts birds from all directions, some to take a deliberate rest stop on their migration path while others are blown in by weather systems moving off the east coast of North America. This explains the large number of species recorded relative to our land mass; nearly 400 species overall, with over 200 species recorded on average yearly.

The island has only 17 permanent breeding species, of which eight are native or endemic, including an endemic sub-species the White-eyed Vireo, known as "Chick-of-the-Village," and two winter visitors who occasionally breed here, the American Coots and the Pied-billed Grebe. Three seabird species visit Bermuda to breed, including our national bird, the endangered endemic Bermuda Petrel (Cahow), and the iconic White-tailed Tropicbird (Longtail) of which Bermuda has the largest breeding colony in the Atlantic.

The best birdwatching location is Spittal Pond, where habitat variety makes it attractive for many species of birds. Cooper's Island Nature Reserve, with its entrance opposite Clearwater Beach, also covers a variety of habits and species as the trail takes you along woodlands, the shoreline, a tidal pond, and a beach. Further along this path is a sheltered cove, at the point called Cooper's Point, which is the best location to see Cahows (Bermuda Petrel), especially in late November.

For information about Bermuda's bird and best birdwatching locations, check out the Bermuda

Audubon Society. Their calendar of events notes birding field trips and photography group outings. The Bermuda Aquarium, Museum & Zoo organizes boat trips to Nonsuch Island, one of the most important sites in Bermuda for rare and threatened species and habitats conservation.

Juvenile heron at Waterville

33. WORLD CLASS SPORTING EVENTS

Bermuda is the perfect location for world class sporting event, not only because of its temperate weather and natural beauty but also because of its accessibility from North America and Europe. Top events on the calendar include the World Triathlon Championship Series, SailGP, the Bermuda Triangle Challenge, and the World Rugby Classic.

The top-tiered leg of the World Triathlon Championship Series with the best triathletes in the world compete in Bermuda in early November. Fellow Bermudians cheer the island's first-ever Olympic Gold Medal Champion, Flora Duffy, creating an even more connected atmosphere.

SailGP is an international sailing competition in May whereby the sport's best athletes, including Olympic gold medallists and world champions, compete using the world's fastest high performance F50 catamarans. SailGP is the most exciting racing on-water, and ideally suited for Bermuda's pleasant climate and impressive courses.

The Bermuda Triangle Challenge is a 3-day running event held in January with three major races involving over 1,500 participants, most from overseas, including invited elite athletes and amateur runners signing up for the experience. On Friday night, the Front Street begins with the Front Street Mile. Saturday morning is the 10k walk/ run, and on Sunday the Bermuda Marathon or Half Marathon. Choose to run the Half Bermuda Triangle Challenge or the Full Bermuda Triangle Challenge - the difference being the marathon distance. Both marathon courses are World Athletics certified and the Bermuda Marathon is a Boston Marathon qualifier.

The World Rugby Classic is a week-long international competition held in November that is unique to Bermuda. Since 1988, the world's top rugby players have been coming to Bermuda for the competition and to mix with fellow international players. In true island style, the event is just as much about comradery, parties, concerts, and welcoming visitors as it is about rugby. Even if you don't understand rugby, this action-packed week is entertaining.

SIGN UP FOR LOCAL EVENTS

34. CHARITY FUNDRAISER WALK/ RUN EVENTS

For visitors wanting to contribute to the wellbeing of the Bermuda community while enjoying the natural beauty of the island, mixing with locals, and getting exercise, the Bermuda calendar includes many walk/ run fundraisers supported enthusiastically by locals and visitors alike. Three of the top fundraiser events visitors may consider joining are the Bermuda End-to-End, Partner Re Women's 5k Walk/ Run, and the BF&M Breast Cancer Awareness Walk.

The Bermuda End-to-End is a mega-event usually held in May. Thousands of participants walk, run, cycle, swim, kayak, or even wheelchair from one end of the island to the other. Support teams providing refreshments, entertainment, and medical attention if needed, line the 25-mile route from St. George's to Dockyard, or the 14-mile Middle-to-End route from Albuoy's Point in Hamilton for those not comfortable with the longer route. Some fun walkers join close to Dockyard to experience the atmosphere and give support to the participants. Overseas visitors are welcome. All participants must register online ahead of the event.

The Partner Re Women's 5k Walk/ Run is one of the few women-only sporting events in the Bermuda calendar. The goal is women's fitness, health, safety, and self-esteem. All proceeds of the event go to women's causes in Bermuda, each year focused on a different charitable organisation. The event takes place in October. Overseas visitors are welcome to sign up for the event and are eligible to win prizes.

BF&M Breast Cancer Awareness Walk, open to men and women, is a 5k walk held mid-October to highlight Breast Cancer Awareness month. Overseas visitors are welcome to sign up.

35. ENTER THE BERMUDA DAY HALF MARATHON DERBY

A Bermuda tradition dating back to 1909, the Bermuda Day Half Marathon Derby is one of the island's longest standing races. Visitors can join the nearly 600 runners from all walks of life who want to accomplish this rite-of-passage. Visitors are not eligible to win prizes. Check out the website www.Bermudamarathon. bm to sign up.

THE ARTS

36. BERMUDA NATIONAL GALLERY

In the City Hall & Arts Centre in Hamilton, the Bermuda National Gallery provides a national platform for Bermudian art and artists, showcasing their work alongside international exhibits. The Bermuda Biennial exhibit, a themed and juried event open May through September during biennial years, shines an international spotlight on our people, our places, our stories, and our future. The gallery hosts a range of engaging exhibits, events, and programs for all ages.

37. A PHOTOGRAPHER'S HAVEN

Chubb office building in Hamilton

The shimmering quality of the light, the vibrant colours of nature, and the pastel-coloured buildings with whitewashed roofs make for picture perfect photos wherever you turn in Bermuda. Whether you're carrying expensive camera equipment or using your smart phone to capture instagrammable moments, there are many great photos to capture.

St. George's is great for photos of winding alleyways, whitewashed historic buildings with dark green wood trim, locals sitting in King's Square under palm-thatched shade, unusual walls, and charming cottages. The roofless ruins of a neo-Gothic stone church, partially built in the late 1800s but never completed, is a great spot for photos.

The Unfinished Church in St. George's

Hamilton's modern architecture and streets also provide interesting photos. The pastel colours of the buildings, the straight lines of the architecture intersecting with the whitewashed roofs, and bright awnings are picture worthy. Don't miss the iconic birdcage at the junction of Front Street and Queen

Street, which was formerly used by Bermuda police to direct traffic. Another photo to capture is Chancery Lane at dusk with its vibrant graffiti on the steps and strings of market lights.

To capture a 360º view of the island, climb the Gibbs Hill Lighthouse in Southampton. You'll see across the Great Sound and down the South Shore.

The Bermuda moongate is iconic. A moongate photo with the ocean in the background is magical. Legend says that if a newlywed couple steps through a moongate holding hands, happiness will endure. You can find moongates on garden walls and at several hotel properties such as Hamilton Princess, Grotto Bay, the Reefs, Cambridge, and Pompano.

You can capture great photos in and around the many forts located island wide. The canons, ramparts, and thick walls of our historic forts make for interesting pictures.

Of course, every beach, Nature Reserve, park, and rock on the shore makes for great photos. Have fun and be creative. There is an abundance of photo opportunities in Bermuda.

38. MASTERWORKS BERMUDA

The Masterworks Museum of Bermuda Art, in a 150-year-old converted arrowroot factory building in the Botanical Gardens, houses over 1,500 Bermuda-inspired art dating from the 1700s to modern day. The most internationally recognisable artist in the collection is Georgia O'Keeffe, who spent a year in Bermuda in the 1930s. There are three galleries displaying permanent collections of paintings, photographs, drawings, maps, sculptures, and other memorabilia. Regular exhibits showcase the work of local artists. The Masterworks Museum of Bermuda Art is for a must for art lovers.

OTHER ACTIVITIES

39. VISIT THE BERMUDA AQUARIUM, MUSEUM & ZOO

The Bermuda Aquarium, Museum & Zoo houses one of the world's oldest aquariums, founded in 1926, and one of our favourite attractions, engaging both locals and visitors alike. On the waterfront at Flatts Village, the facility is also an important centre for science education, research, and species conservation.

Plan to spend 2 to 3 hours to explore all three unique attractions within the complex - the aquarium, the natural history museum, and the zoo. Perfect for an afternoon entertaining children and grandchildren.

Across the road from the Bermuda Aquarium, Museum & Zoo

40. LOCAL CRAFTS AT HARBOUR NIGHTS

Harbour Nights Street Festival is a street celebration every Wednesday night during the high season (May to November). Front Street in Hamilton is closed to vehicular traffic after sunset, and shops remain open late, as do restaurants.

Front Street comes alive with the sights, aromas, and sounds of Harbour Night's festive atmosphere set with the backdrop of the illuminated harbour. Large numbers of vendors sell a variety of local arts and crafts. The artists and craftspeople are delighted to chat with you and explain their artwork. There are also many food vendors selling Bermudian and ethnic food. Children enjoy all the activities in the children's court, such as fun castles, face-painting, temporary tattoos, the popular train, and hair braiding. And of course, there are local entertainers, including musicians, DJs, the Bermuda Regiment band with pipes and drums, and showcase performances by iconic Bermuda Gombey troupes.

This outstanding event for all ages provides insight into the Bermudian way of life.

Be sure to book dinner reservations in Hamilton. The restaurants are typically busier on Harbour Nights, especially ones with the best vantage points to watch the street festival. Some favourites with balconies overlooking the Front Street are The Pickled Onion, The Terrace, Flanigan's Irish Pub & Restaurant, Pearl, and Bolero Brasserie. Restaurants with patios on street level include The Front Yard, The Astwood Arms, Port O Call, and Bermuda Bistro.

41. A WHALE OF A TIME

Whale watching in Bermuda is an experience of a lifetime. If you are here in the spring, we recommend you take part in the spring ritual of whale-watching off the south shore of the island.

There are three separate populations of Humpback whales worldwide. One group is in the oceans of the South Hemisphere, and another group is in the North Pacific. The third is in the North Atlantic. Bermuda is halfway between the feeding grounds and the wintering and breeding grounds of the North Atlantic humpback whale population.

About fifteen thousand humpback whales of the North Atlantic population migrate over 3,100 miles from the warm Caribbean waters to the cooler waters and better feeding grounds of New England, the Maritime provinces of Canada, Labrador, Greenland, Iceland and even Norway. Many of the migrating North Atlantic population pass through Bermuda waters off the south shore in March and April.

The best way to see these majestic animals is to join an organised whale watching boat tour. There are several operators in Bermuda who can take you out to the south shore waters for several hours of whale watching. The Bermuda Underwater Exploration Institute, on the outskirts of Hamilton, run tours every Saturday, Sunday, and Wednesday between mid-March and mid-April.

Humpback whale on south shore courtesy of Graham Jack

North Atlantic humpback whale population migration, there is world-class research in Bermuda you can tap into. As a mid-ocean seamount rising above the surface of the water, Bermuda is a perfect base for research into the migratory behaviour of humpback whales. For information about The Humpback Whale Film & Research Project, started in 2007 by Andrew Stevenson to study the humpbacks as they migrate past Bermuda and to document their lives with underwater, high-definition video footage and hydrophone recordings, check out www.whalesbermuda.com and www.bamz.org/conserve/humpback-whale-project for information.

42. BERMUDA GLOW WORM MATING RITUAL

The chance to witness bioluminescence, which is the production and emission of light by a living organism, inspires child-like glee, and we remember vividly our first encounter with the phenomenon, whether on land (fireflies) or in the ocean (jellyfish). There are no fireflies in Bermuda. We have a special source of bioluminescence in our waters to be appreciated with child-like glee.

The Bermuda fireworm, or glow worm as we call it, inhabits shallow areas of the western Atlantic Ocean. The worm is bioluminescent when it rises to the surface during its mating period.

These tiny creatures makes a big impact using chemical reaction to produce light to attract a mate. The worms reproduce by external fertilisation, and both the female eggs and the male gametes appear bright green when released in the water.

The mating ritual of the Bermuda glow worm is very precise. Likely it's the most precise thing on our island, where "Bermuda time" is relaxed. Two days after the full moon, at exactly 56 minutes after sunset, we can observe their spectacular light show.

You can watch from the shore at shallow, sandy-bottomed areas such as Ferry Point Park, Flatts Inlet, Mangrove Bay, and Ely's Harbour. To view it from the water, there are several tour operators advertising glow worm cruises.

43. SWIM WITH THE DOLPHINS

Dolphin Quest uniquely provides direct connection to dolphins, marine life, and the ocean through feedings, trainer workshops, and swimming sessions in a dolphin enclosure at a dockside complex. Dolphin Quest is in a historic fort, now known as the National Museum of Bermuda at Dockyard, the perfect backdrop to enhance the experience.

While you are in the National Museum, explore the historic grounds, the many exhibits, and the playhouse/ playground for children.

44. BERMUDA UNDERWATER EXPLORATION INSTITUTE

The Bermuda Underwater Exploration Institute (BUEI) is a modern and innovative 41,000-square-foot discovery centre on the outskirts of Hamilton focused on advancing everyone's knowledge of our oceans and seas and bringing a unique experience to people of all ages. With three floors of exhibits,

121

many of them interactive and playful, it's the perfect place for families with young children or anyone interested in learning about the vast and diverse marine environment around the island.

BUEI has an enormous collection of artifacts and priceless treasures retrieved from the ocean floor thanks to the late Teddy Tucker, a renowned Bermudian wreck diver who discovered over 100 shipwrecks around the island. There's also one of the world's largest private shell collections, a floor devoted to the underwater geology, a darkened exhibit on bioluminescence and the marine organisms that create it, and an immersive exhibit employing innovative technology to enable visitors to explore both the far-fetched theories and the science behind Bermuda's most intriguing mystery - the Bermuda Triangle.

45. IF IN DOUBT, CHECK THE RADAR BEFORE HEADING OUT

Bright blue skies are the norm, but the weather can be quirky, showering one parish with a windy downpour and the adjacent parish with sunshine.

We understand the trade-offs in Bermuda; the trade winds make for great sailing, and the rainfall throughout the year keeps our parks, nature reserves, and golf courses lush. Unlike some island destinations, Bermuda does not have a rainy season. Heavier downpours typically occur during the night, and don't last long.

When we have plans for outdoor recreational activity and the weather looks threatening, we check the Bermuda Service Doppler Weather Radar provided by the Bermuda Airport Authority. The radar provides an immediate view of the weather approaching or currently over the island through SRI (Surface Rainfall Intensity) animation. There are three map views, one showing 62 miles around the island, one showing 155 miles, and one showing the

SRI at the parish level. Go to the website
www.weather.bm/radar.asp.

46. TURN ON THE RADIO FOR THE BERMUDA ISLAND VIBE

Music can tell you about a place. When in Bermuda, check out the live music hotspots to hear our best musicians. But before you come, or even when chilling around the pool of your Bermuda home share accommodation, tune into Bermuda's radio stations streaming online (Online Radio Box) for a taste of island vibe.

The Captain on Ocean FM 89 showcases dance music, top 40, and news; Irie FM 98.3 is all about reggae music; Miss Thang on Power FM 95 will give you the scoop; DJ Chubb on Vibe FM 103 brings you the latest soca, R&B, and reggae; Magic FM 102.7 brings you talk shows such as the latest of what's new in Bermuda.

47. FERRY RIDE AROUND THE GREAT SOUND

Our SeaExpress Ferry service is a convenient method of transportation for locals and visitors. It's an inexpensive way to take in the sights from the water.

The ferry terminal is on Front Street near Albuoy's Point in Hamilton. The ferry schedule has three different routes traversing the Great Sound, the large body of water that forms our natural harbour. The Blue Route provides direct service between Hamilton and Dockyard; Pink Route services Paget and Warwick, with five stops on the round trip from Hamilton; and Green Route stops at Watford Bridge, Cavello Bay, and Rockaway. You can get the latest schedule from the ferry terminal or online.

48. PURCHASE A DAY PASS AT A RESORT

If you want to enhance your cruise holiday or lose yourself at a resort, a day pass is a good option.

The only resort offering day passes with resort access is the Pompano. Pompano is the perfect location to relax poolside or on the beach and enjoy server service for food and beverages right in your deck chair. One advantage for cruise ship passengers is that Pompano is not far from the Dockyard cruise ship terminal. Call or email up to seven days in advance to book your day pass, which depends on the hotel's occupancy.

The Reefs Resort & Club offers day passes to those with spa appointments. The St. Regis Bermuda Resort has day passes for use of spa amenities only.

49. TAKE TIME TO NOTICE THE FRAGRANCE OF THE ISLAND

Lili Bermuda Perfumery

Scent is a powerful link to our memory, tethering us forever to our experiences of a time or a place. When you think about it, scent is the ultimate souvenir, and it's free and readily accessible.

The reason our memories are so strongly associated with scent is because it is the only one of our five senses that goes directly to the region of our brain responsible for emotion and memory.

You can create your smell memory when travelling by being mindful of the surrounding fragrances, and if you smell something interesting, ask a local what it is so you can bookmark the smell in your memory.

The fragrance of Bermuda is primarily thanks to the abundance of flowering trees and shrubs on the island, such as frangipani, jasmine, Natal plum, allspice, pittosporum, Surinam cherries, and mimosa. Freesia blooms, with their strong spicy-sweet fragrance, herald springtime.

If you wish you could take the fragrance of the island in a bottle home with you, visit Lili Bermuda Perfumery. From the pure scent of the wind and fresh salt spray of the ocean to its luscious botanicals such as Bermuda cedarwood, spring freesias and juicy loquats, Lili Bermuda is an artistic reflection of Bermuda where each fragrance represents the island's natural beauty. Visit, take a tour, or even do a workshop to create your signature scent at this iconic gem in St. George's.

50. REACH OUT ON SOCIAL MEDIA

We have an active social media on the island for locals, visitors, and fans of the island. To name a few, check out @Bermemes, @wearebda365, @itskristindotcom, @bermuda, and @foreverbermuda. For specific questions or recommendations, join the Facebook Group "Maj's List." ForeverBermuda is a great resource to find out news from the islands.

BONUS TIP 1. WATCH "FLYING OVER BERMUDA" YOUTUBE VIDEOS

There are several videos on YouTube titled "Flying Over Bermuda," and the one by Nature Relaxation Films, featuring an array of scenic views of Bermuda set to relaxing music, has garnered over 3.4 million views.

BONUS TIP 2. APPLY FOR A BERMUDA DIGITAL VISA: WORK FROM BERMUDA CERTIFICATE

The Bermuda government introduced the Work from Bermuda Certificate to satisfy the growing demand to work remotely in a variety of environments. It allows executives and students to work and study remotely from the island in a beautiful and worry-free environment.

Foreign nationals can apply to live and work here for up to one year. Check the Bermuda Government website for further details and the application form.

The Grotto Bay Beach Resort & Spa have expanded their offerings to cater to visitors looking for long-term accommodation at affordable rates for either weekly or monthly stays.

BONUS TIP 3. SIGN UP FOR BERMUDA. COM NEWSLETTER

Bermuda.com is the ultimate website about events in Bermuda. Keep abreast by signing to have their weekly newsletter delivered directly to your email.

TOP REASONS TO BOOK THIS TRIP

Beaches: The beaches here are the best.

Food: The food is amazing.

Island Culture: A rich heritage of tradition.

DID YOU KNOW?

1. Bermuda comprises seven main islands and about 170 additional named islets and rocks.

2. Early sailors, once scared of the waters and islands around Bermuda, called them the Isle of Devils thanks in part to its loud indigenous birds, the treacherous ring of coral reef encircling it, and the sometimes-stormy weather.

3. Some scholars claim that William Shakespeare's play "The Tempest" was based on the shipwreck of the Sea Venture on Bermuda.

4. Bermuda is an internally self-governing British overseas territory with a parliamentary government. Under its 1968 constitution, the British monarch, represented by the governor, is the head of state.

5. During the American Civil War, Bermuda was a staging area for blockade runners to Southern ports.

6. Portuguese Rock, in Spittal Pond Nature Reserve, is a historic monument marking the spot that's believed to be the earliest human remnants on the island.

7. Bermuda's legal system is based on English common law.

8. The 1968 constitution granted Bermuda autonomy, except for foreign relations, defence, and internal security.

9. Bermuda's nearest landmass is Cape Hatteras, North Carolina, about 640 miles to the west-northwest.

10. Bermuda's terrain comprises primarily low hills and fertile depressions.

RESOURCES:

1. Bermuda Tourism: www.gotobermuda.com

2. Bermuda Events: www.bermuda.com

3. Government of Bermuda: www.gov.bm

4. City of Hamilton: www.cityofhamilton.bm

5. Bermuda National Trust: www.bnt.bm

6. The Bermuda Railway Trail:
   www.bermudarailway.net

7. The Bermuda Audubon Society:
   www.audubon.bm

8. Oxford English Dictionary, Bermudian English:
   https://public.oed.com/blog/introducing-
   bermudian-english
   /

TRIVIA – JUST FOR FUN

1. What is a term given for a Bermudian?

2. What is the smallest national varietal represented in the Oxford English Dictionary?

3. How long does it take to drive from one end of the island to the other?

4. What is the shape of the island?

5. What do locals put on their pies?

6. What 1997 box office thriller was filmed in Bermuda?

7. What does the phrase "De Rock" mean?

8. What items were smuggled into the US from Bermuda in 1919-1933?

9. How many songs did John Lennon complete while in Bermuda?

10. Is Bermuda part of the Caribbean?

ANSWERS

1. Onion

2. Bermudian English

3. 2 hours

4. Fishhook

5. Mayonnaise

6. The Deep

7. Bermuda

8. Liquors of all kinds

9. Over 20

10. No

PACKING AND PLANNING TIPS

A Week before Leaving

- Arrange for someone to take care of pets and water plants.

- Email and Print important Documents.

- Get Visa and vaccines if needed.

- Check for travel warnings.

- Stop mail and newspaper.

- Notify Credit Card companies where you are going.

- Passports and photo identification is up to date.

- Pay bills.

- Copy important items and download travel Apps.

- Start collecting small bills for tips.

- Have post office hold mail while you are away.

- Check weather for the week.

- Car inspected, oil is changed, and tires have the correct pressure.

- Check airline luggage restrictions.

- Download Apps needed for your trip.

Right Before Leaving

- Contact bank and credit cards to tell them your location.

- Clean out refrigerator.

- Empty garbage cans.

- Lock windows.

- Make sure you have the proper identification with you.

- Bring cash for tips.

- Remember travel documents.

- Lock door behind you.

- Remember wallet.

- Unplug items in house and pack chargers.

- Change your thermostat settings.

- Charge electronics, and prepare camera memory cards.

READ OTHER
GREATER THAN A TOURIST
BOOKS

CZYKPublishing.com

METRIC CONVERSIONS

TEMPERATURE

110° F —
100° F —
90° F —
80° F —
70° F —
60° F —
50° F —
40° F —
32° F —
20° F —
10° F —
0° F —
-10° F —
-20° F —

— 40° C
— 30° C
— 20° C
— 10° C
— 0° C
— -10° C
— -18° C
— -30° C

To convert F to C:

Subtract 32, and then multiply by 5/9 or .5555.

To Convert C to F:

Multiply by 1.8 and then add 32.

32F = 0C

LIQUID VOLUME

To Convert:..................Multiply by
U.S. Gallons to Liters................ 3.8
U.S. Liters to Gallons 26
Imperial Gallons to U.S. Gallons 1.2
Imperial Gallons to Liters....... 4.55
Liters to Imperial Gallons 22

1 Liter = .26 U.S. Gallon
1 U.S. Gallon = 3.8 Liters

DISTANCE

To convert ....Multiply by
Inches to Centimeters 2.54
Centimeters to Inches 39
Feet to Meters...................... .3
Meters to Feet 3.28
Yards to Meters 91
Meters to Yards 1.09
Miles to Kilometers 1.61
Kilometers to Miles............ .62

1 Mile = 1.6 km
1 km = .62 Miles

WEIGHT

1 Ounce = .28 Grams
1 Pound = .4555 Kilograms
1 Gram = .04 Ounce
1 Kilogram = 2.2 Pounds

143

TRAVEL QUESTIONS

- Do you bring presents home to family or friends after a vacation?

- Do you get motion sick?

- Do you have a favorite billboard?

- Do you know what to do if there is a flat tire?

- Do you like a sun roof open?

- Do you like to eat in the car?

- Do you like to wear sun glasses in the car?

- Do you like toppings on your ice cream?

- Do you use public bathrooms?

- Did you bring a cell phone and does it have power?

- Do you have a form of identification with you?

- Have you ever been pulled over by a cop?

- Have you ever given money to a stranger on a road trip?

- Have you ever taken a road trip with animals?

- Have you ever gone on a vacation alone?

- Have you ever run out of gas?

- If you could move to any place in the world, where would it be?

- If you could travel anywhere in the world, where would you travel?

- If you could travel in any vehicle, which one would it be?

- If you had three things to wish for from a magic genie, what would they be?

- If you have a driver's license, how many times did it take you to pass the test?

- What are you the most afraid of on vacation?

- What do you want to get away from the most when you are on vacation?

- What foods smell bad to you?

- What item do you bring on ever trip with you away from home?

- What makes you sleepy?

- What song would you love to hear on the radio when you're cruising on the highway?

- What travel job would you want the least?

- What will you miss most while you are away from home?

- What is something you always wanted to try?

- What is the best road side attraction that you ever saw?

- What is the farthest distance you ever biked?

- What is the farthest distance you ever walked?

- What is the weirdest thing you needed to buy while on vacation?

- What is your favorite candy?

- What is your favorite color car?

- What is your favorite family vacation?

- What is your favorite food?

- What is your favorite gas station drink or food?

- What is your favorite license plate design?

- What is your favorite restaurant?

- What is your favorite smell?

- What is your favorite song?

- What is your favorite sound that nature makes?

- What is your favorite thing to bring home from a vacation?

- What is your favorite vacation with friends?

- What is your favorite way to relax?

- Where is the farthest place you ever traveled in a car?

- Where is the farthest place you ever went North, South, East and West?

- Where is your favorite place in the world?

- Who is your favorite singer?

- Who taught you how to drive?

- Who will you miss the most while you are away?

- Who if the first person you will contact when you get to your destination?

- Who brought you on your first vacation?

- Who likes to travel the most in your life?

- Would you rather be hot or cold?

- Would you rather drive above, below, or at the speed limited?

- Would you rather drive on a highway or a back road?

- Would you rather go on a train or a boat?

- Would you rather go to the beach or the woods?

TRAVEL BUCKET LIST

1.

2.

3.

4.

5.

6.

7.

8.

9.

10.

Made in the USA
Monee, IL
05 March 2023